Simple & Delicious

PASTA

Simple & Delicious

PASTA

OVER 100 SENSATIONAL RECIPES FOR PASTA LOVERS

This edition published in 2013
LOVE FOOD is an imprint of Parragon Books Ltd

Parragon
Chartist House
15–17 Trim Street
Bath, BA1 1HA, UK

LOVE FOOD and the accompanying heart device is a registered trade mark of Parragon Books Ltd in Australia, the UK, USA, India and the EU.

www.parragon.com/lovefood

ISBN: 978-1-78186-777-8

Printed in China

Cover design by Geoff Borin
Internal photography by Günter Beer and Don Last
Additional home economy by Oliver Trific and Christine France
Introduction by Anne Sheasby

Notes for the Reader
This book uses both metric and imperial measurements. Follow the same units of measurement throughout; do not mix metric and imperial. All spoon measurements are level: teaspoons are assumed to be 5 ml, and tablespoons are assumed to be 15 ml. Unless otherwise stated, milk is assumed to be full fat, eggs and individual vegetables are medium, and pepper is freshly ground black pepper. Unless otherwise stated, all root vegetables should be washed in plain water and peeled prior to using.

For best results, use a food thermometer when cooking meat and poultry – check the latest government guidelines for current advice.

Garnishes, decorations and serving suggestions are all optional and not necessarily included in the recipe ingredients or method.

The times given are an approximate guide only. Preparation times differ according to the techniques used by different people and the cooking times may also vary from those given. Optional ingredients, variations or serving suggestions have not been included in the time calculations.

Recipes using raw or very lightly cooked eggs should be avoided by infants, the elderly, pregnant women, convalescents and anyone suffering from an illness. Pregnant and breastfeeding women are advised to avoid eating peanuts and peanut products. Sufferers from nut allergies should be aware that some of the ready-made ingredients used in the recipes in this book may contain nuts. Always check the packaging before use.

Vegetarians should be aware that some of the ready-made ingredients used in the recipes in this book may contain animal products. Always check the packaging before use.

Contents

Introduction

Pasta has played an important role in the Italian diet for centuries, but it has also become a very popular food in many countries across the globe. Pasta is a versatile, convenient and economical food. It is easy to prepare, quick to cook and can be combined with all sorts of ingredients to create a tempting range of dishes to suit all tastes.

The word *pasta* literally means 'dough' or 'paste'. The best fresh pastas are made from a basic combination of type/grade '00' pasta flour, eggs, salt and sometimes a little olive oil and/or water. Top quality dried pastas are made from 100 per cent durum (hard, high-protein) wheat, and some include the addition of eggs. Other ingredients, such as spinach, garlic and chopped herbs, tomato purée, squid ink, mushrooms, beetroot, saffron etc, may be added to the basic pasta dough to add flavour and colour.

The variety of both fresh and dried pastas available is extensive and includes long pasta (such as spaghetti, tagliatelle and linguine), short pasta (such as penne, macaroni and fusilli) or more unusual shapes (such as conchiglie, radiatori or lumache). Other varieties include soup pasta (*pastina* or 'little pasta') and stuffed pasta (such as ravioli). Lasagne sheets and cannelloni tubes are used in baked pasta dishes.

Storing Pasta

Dried pasta is a convenient store-cupboard standby as it has a long shelf life. Dried pasta should be stored in an airtight container in a cool, dry place. Keep an eye on the 'best-before' date on the packaging.

Fresh pasta on the other hand is best used immediately or stored in an airtight container in the refrigerator and used within 2 days. Cooked, cooled pasta should be kept in a sealed container in the refrigerator and used within 2 days.

Plain cooked pasta does not freeze well on its own, but it does freeze successfully in dishes such as lasagne. Uncooked fresh pasta freezes well in a covered container or sealed polythene freezer bag for up to 1 month, and it can be cooked from frozen.

Cooking Pasta

Pasta should always be cooked in a large pan containing plenty of boiling, salted water. It should be added to fast-boiling water and the water should be kept at a rolling boil throughout cooking. Stir the pasta when you initially add it to the water, then quickly bring it to the boil again and continue to cook the pasta uncovered, stirring occasionally.

You can add a dash of oil to the water if you wish. Some believe that the addition of oil helps to prevent the pasta from sticking together, but it is not strictly necessary.

Fresh unfilled pasta takes about 1–3 minutes to cook and fresh filled pasta takes about 3–4 minutes to cook, depending on the variety. Dried unfilled pasta takes between 8–10 minutes to cook, and dried filled pasta takes between 10–15 minutes to cook, depending on the variety.

Cooked pasta should be *al dente*, which means that it should be tender but still have a slight resistance to the bite. As soon as the pasta is cooked, drain it thoroughly through a colander or large strainer, shaking off any excess water, then quickly toss it with the prepared sauce or ingredients. Serve the hot pasta immediately on warmed plates or in warmed bowls.

If you are serving the cooked pasta cold, for example in a pasta salad, rinse the pasta under cold running water to stop any further cooking, then drain it well. Toss the cold pasta with a little olive oil or salad dressing to prevent the pieces sticking together, then chill until required.

Serving Pasta

Choosing which pasta to serve with a particular sauce is often a matter of personal taste but the following general guidelines may help.

Small pasta tubes and twists, such as penne (quills), farfalle (bow ties) and fusilli (spirals), are ideal for chunky vegetable- or meat-based sauces. Larger pasta tubes, such as rigatoni, are good for some meat sauces.

Smooth-textured, cream-, butter- or olive oil-based sauces or meat sauces, are ideal for long strands of pasta, such as spaghetti, tagliatelle, linguine or fettuccine. The sauce should be able to cling to the long pasta when it is twirled onto a fork.

Lasagne, cannelloni and macaroni work best when baked in recipes.

The smallest pasta shapes are ideal for adding texture and interest to soups.

Soups &
Salads

Minestrone

serves 4

2 tbsp olive oil

2 garlic cloves, chopped

2 red onions, chopped

75 g/2¾ oz Parma ham, sliced

1 red pepper, deseeded and chopped

1 orange pepper, deseeded and chopped

400 g/14 oz canned chopped tomatoes

1 litre/1¾ pints vegetable stock

1 celery stick, chopped

400 g/14 oz canned borlotti beans

100 g/3½ oz green leafy cabbage, shredded

75 g/2¾ oz frozen peas, defrosted

1 tbsp chopped fresh parsley

75 g/2¾ oz dried vermicelli

salt and pepper

freshly grated Parmesan cheese, to garnish

Heat the oil in a large saucepan. Add the garlic, onions and Parma ham and cook over a medium heat, stirring, for 3 minutes, until slightly softened. Add the red and orange peppers and the chopped tomatoes and cook for a further 2 minutes, stirring. Stir in the stock, then add the celery. Drain and add the borlotti beans along with the cabbage, peas and parsley. Season to taste with salt and pepper. Bring to the boil, then lower the heat and simmer for 30 minutes.

Add the vermicelli to the pan. Cook for a further 4–5 minutes, or according to the instructions on the packet. Remove from the heat and ladle into warmed serving bowls. Garnish with freshly grated Parmesan and serve immediately.

Brown Lentil & Pasta Soup

serves 4

4 rashers streaky bacon, cut into small squares

1 onion, chopped

2 garlic cloves, crushed

2 celery sticks, chopped

50 g/1¾ oz dried farfalline

400 g/14 oz canned brown lentils, drained

1.2 litres/2 pints vegetable stock

2 tbsp chopped fresh mint

fresh mint sprigs, to garnish

Place the bacon in a large frying pan together with the onion, garlic and celery. Dry fry for 4–5 minutes, stirring, until the onion is tender and the bacon is just beginning to brown.

Add the pasta to the frying pan and cook, stirring, for 1 minute to coat the pasta in the fat.

Add the lentils and the vegetable stock and bring to the boil. Reduce the heat and leave to simmer for 8–10 minutes, or until the pasta is tender but still firm to the bite.

Remove the frying pan from the heat and stir in the chopped fresh mint. Transfer the soup to warmed soup bowls, garnish with fresh mint sprigs and serve immediately.

Tuscan Bean Soup

serves 6

300 g/10½ oz canned cannellini beans, drained and rinsed

300 g/10½ oz canned borlotti beans, drained and rinsed

about 600 ml/1 pint chicken or vegetable stock

115 g/4 oz dried macaroni

4–5 tbsp olive oil

2 garlic cloves, very finely chopped

3 tbsp chopped fresh flat-leaf parsley

salt and pepper

Place half the cannellini and half the borlotti beans in a food processor with half the stock and process until smooth. Pour into a large, heavy-based saucepan and add the remaining beans. Stir in enough of the remaining stock to achieve the consistency you like, then bring to the boil.

Add the pasta and return to the boil, then reduce the heat and cook for 8–10 minutes, or until just tender.

Meanwhile, heat 3 tablespoons of the oil in a small frying pan. Add the garlic and cook, stirring constantly, for 2–3 minutes, or until golden. Stir the garlic into the soup with the parsley.

Season to taste with salt and pepper and ladle into warmed soup bowls. Drizzle with the remaining olive oil to taste and serve immediately.

Potato & Pesto Soup

serves 4

2 tbsp olive oil

2 rashers rindless smoked
bacon, finely chopped

25 g/1 oz butter

450 g/1 lb floury potatoes,
chopped

450 g/1 lb onions, finely
chopped

600 ml/1 pint chicken stock

600 ml/1 pint milk

100 g/3½ oz dried
conchigliette

150 ml/5 fl oz double cream

2 tbsp pesto

2 tbsp chopped parsley

salt and pepper

freshly grated Parmesan
cheese, to serve

Heat the oil in a large saucepan and cook the bacon over a medium heat for 4 minutes. Add the butter, potatoes and onions and cook for 12 minutes, stirring constantly.

Add the stock and milk to the saucepan, bring to the boil and simmer for 10 minutes. Add the pasta and simmer for a further 3–4 minutes.

Blend in the cream and simmer for 5 minutes. Add the pesto and chopped parsley and season to taste with salt and pepper. Transfer the soup to individual serving bowls and serve with Parmesan cheese.

Fresh Tomato Soup

serves 4

1 tbsp olive oil

650 g/1 lb 7 oz plum tomatoes

1 onion, cut into quarters

1 garlic clove, sliced thinly

1 celery stick, coarsely chopped

500 ml/18 fl oz chicken stock

55 g/2 oz dried anellini or other soup pasta

salt and pepper

chopped fresh flat-leaf parsley, to garnish

Heat the oil in a large, heavy-based saucepan and add the tomatoes, onion, garlic and celery. Cover and cook over a low heat for 45 minutes, occasionally shaking the saucepan gently, until the mixture is pulpy.

Transfer the mixture to a food processor or blender and process to a smooth purée. Push the purée through a sieve into a clean saucepan.

Add the stock and bring to the boil. Add the pasta, bring back to the boil and cook for 8–10 minutes, until the pasta is tender but still firm to the bite. Season to taste with salt and pepper. Ladle into warmed bowls, sprinkle with the parsley and serve immediately.

Italian Chicken Soup

serves 4

450 g/1 lb skinless, boneless chicken breast, cut into thin strips

1.2 litres/2 pints chicken stock

150 ml/5 fl oz double cream

115 g/4 oz dried vermicelli

1 tbsp cornflour

3 tbsp milk

175 g/6 oz canned sweetcorn kernels, drained

salt and pepper

Place the chicken in a large saucepan and pour in the chicken stock and cream. Bring to the boil, then reduce the heat and simmer for 20 minutes.

Meanwhile, bring a large, heavy-based saucepan of lightly salted water to the boil. Add the pasta, return to the boil and cook for 4–5 minutes, or until just tender but still firm to the bite. Drain the pasta well and keep warm.

Season the soup to taste with salt and pepper. Mix the cornflour and milk together until a smooth paste forms, then stir it into the soup. Add the sweetcorn and pasta and heat through. Ladle the soup into warmed soup bowls and serve.

Chicken & Chickpea Soup

serves 4

2 tbsp butter

3 spring onions, chopped

2 garlic cloves, crushed

1 sprig of fresh marjoram, finely chopped

350 g/12 oz chicken breasts, diced

1.2 litres/2 pints chicken stock

350 g/12 oz canned chickpeas, drained and rinsed

1 bouquet garni

1 red pepper, diced

1 green pepper, diced

115 g/4 oz dried macaroni

salt and white pepper

croûtons, to garnish

Melt the butter in a large pan over a medium heat. Add the spring onions, garlic, marjoram and chicken and cook, stirring frequently, for 5 minutes.

Add the chicken stock, chickpeas and bouquet garni. Season to taste with salt and white pepper.

Bring the soup to the boil over a medium heat. Reduce the heat and simmer for about 2 hours.

Add the diced peppers and pasta to the pan, then simmer for a further 20 minutes.

Ladle the soup into warmed serving bowls and garnish with croûtons. Serve immediately.

Tuscan Veal Broth

serves 4

55 g/2 oz dried peas, soaked for 2 hours and drained

900 g/2 lb boned neck of veal, diced

1.2 litres/2 pints beef stock

600 ml/1 pint water

55 g/2 oz pearl barley, rinsed and drained

1 large carrot, diced

1 small turnip (about 175 g/ 6 oz), diced

1 large leek, thinly sliced

1 red onion, finely chopped

100 g/3½ oz chopped tomatoes

1 sprig of fresh basil

100 g/3½ oz dried vermicelli

salt and white pepper

Put the peas, veal, stock and water into a large pan and bring to the boil over a low heat. Using a slotted spoon, skim off any scum that rises to the surface.

When all of the scum has been removed, add the pearl barley and a pinch of salt to the mixture. Simmer gently over a low heat for 25 minutes.

Add the carrot, turnip, leek, onion, tomatoes and basil to the pan, and season to taste with salt and pepper. Leave to simmer for about 2 hours, skimming the surface from time to time to remove any scum. Remove the pan from the heat and set aside for 2 hours.

Set the pan over a medium heat and bring to the boil. Add the vermicelli and cook for 4–5 minutes. Season to taste with salt and pepper, then remove and discard the basil. Ladle into soup bowls and serve immediately.

Fish Soup with Macaroni

serves 6

2 tbsp olive oil

2 onions, sliced

1 garlic clove, finely chopped

1 litre/1¾ pints fish stock or water

400 g/14 oz canned chopped tomatoes

¼ tsp herbes de Provence

¼ tsp saffron threads

115 g/4 oz dried macaroni

18 live mussels, scrubbed and debearded

450 g/1 lb monkfish fillet, cut into chunks

225 g/8 oz raw prawns, peeled and deveined, tails left on

salt and pepper

Heat the oil in a large, heavy-based saucepan. Add the onions and garlic and cook over a low heat, stirring occasionally, for 5 minutes, or until the onions have softened.

Add the fish stock with the tomatoes and their can juices, herbs, saffron and pasta and season to taste with salt and pepper. Bring to the boil, then cover and simmer for 15 minutes.

Discard any mussels with broken shells or any that refuse to close when tapped. Add the mussels, monkfish and prawns to the saucepan. Re-cover the saucepan and simmer for a further 5–10 minutes, until the mussels have opened, the prawns have changed colour and the fish is opaque and flakes easily. Discard any mussels that remain closed. Ladle the soup into warmed bowls and serve.

Warm Pasta Salad

serves 4

225 g/8 oz dried farfalle

6 pieces of sun-dried tomato in oil, drained and chopped

4 spring onions, chopped

55 g/2 oz rocket, shredded

½ cucumber, deseeded and diced

salt and pepper

freshly grated Parmesan cheese, to serve

for the dressing

4 tbsp olive oil

1 tbsp white wine vinegar

½ tsp caster sugar

1 tsp Dijon mustard

4 fresh basil leaves, finely shredded

salt and pepper

To make the dressing, whisk the oil, vinegar, sugar and mustard together in a jug. Season to taste with salt and pepper and stir in the basil.

Bring a large, heavy-based saucepan of lightly salted water to the boil. Add the pasta, return to the boil and cook for 8–10 minutes, or until tender but still firm to the bite. Drain and transfer to a salad bowl. Add the dressing and toss well.

Add the tomatoes, spring onions, rocket and cucumber, season to taste with salt and pepper and toss. Sprinkle with the Parmesan cheese and serve warm.

Pasta Salad with Walnuts & Dolcelatte

serves 4

225 g/8 oz dried farfalle

2 tbsp walnut oil

4 tbsp safflower oil

2 tbsp balsamic vinegar

280 g/10 oz mixed salad leaves

225 g/8 oz dolcelatte cheese, diced

115 g/4 oz walnuts, halved and toasted

salt and pepper

Bring a large, heavy-based saucepan of lightly salted water to the boil. Add the pasta, return to the boil and cook for 8–10 minutes, or until tender but still firm to the bite. Drain and refresh in a bowl of cold water. Drain again.

Mix the walnut oil, safflower oil and vinegar together in a jug, whisking well, and season to taste with salt and pepper.

Arrange the salad leaves in a large serving bowl. Top with the pasta, dolcelatte cheese and walnuts. Pour the dressing over the salad, toss lightly and serve.

Penne & Apple Salad

serves 4

2 large lettuces

250 g/9 oz dried penne

1 tbsp olive oil

8 red apples, diced

juice of 4 lemons

1 head of celery, sliced

115 g/4 oz walnut halves

250 ml/9 fl oz fresh garlic
mayonnaise

salt and pepper

Wash, drain and pat dry the lettuce leaves with kitchen paper. Transfer them to the refrigerator for 1 hour, or until crisp.

Meanwhile, bring a large saucepan of lightly salted water to the boil. Add the pasta and olive oil, bring back to the boil and cook for 8–10 minutes, or until tender but still firm to the bite. Drain the pasta and refresh under cold running water. Drain thoroughly and cool.

Core and dice the apples, place them in a bowl and sprinkle with the lemon juice to coat them thoroughly – this will prevent them from turning brown. Mix together the cold pasta, sliced celery, diced apples and walnut halves and toss the mixture in the garlic mayonnaise. Season to taste with salt and pepper.

Line a salad bowl with the lettuce leaves and spoon the pasta salad on top. Chill until required.

Pasta Salad with Chargrilled Peppers

serves 4

1 red pepper

1 orange pepper

280 g/10 oz dried conchiglie

5 tbsp extra virgin olive oil

2 tbsp lemon juice

2 tbsp pesto

1 garlic clove, crushed

3 tbsp shredded fresh basil leaves

salt and pepper

Put the whole peppers on a baking sheet and place under a preheated grill, turning frequently, for 15 minutes, until charred all over. Remove with tongs and place in a bowl. Cover with crumpled kitchen paper and set aside.

Meanwhile, bring a large saucepan of lightly salted water to the boil. Add the pasta, bring back to the boil and cook for 8–10 minutes, until tender but still firm to the bite.

Combine the olive oil, lemon juice, pesto and garlic in a bowl, whisking well to mix. Drain the pasta, add it to the pesto mixture while still hot and toss well. Set aside.

When the peppers are cool enough to handle, peel off the skins, then cut open and remove the seeds. Chop the flesh coarsely and add to the pasta with the basil. Season to taste with salt and pepper and toss well. Serve at room temperature.

Rare Beef Pasta Salad

serves 4

450 g/1 lb rump or sirloin steak in 1 piece

450 g/1 lb dried fusilli

4 tbsp olive oil

2 tbsp lime juice

2 tbsp Thai fish sauce

2 tsp clear honey

4 spring onions, sliced

1 cucumber, peeled and cut into 2.5-cm/1-inch chunks

3 tomatoes, cut into wedges

3 tsp finely chopped fresh mint

salt and pepper

Season the steak to taste with salt and pepper, then grill or pan-fry for 4 minutes on each side. Leave to rest for 5 minutes, then, using a sharp knife, slice the steak thinly across the grain and reserve until required.

Meanwhile, bring a large pan of lightly salted water to the boil over a medium heat. Add the pasta, bring back to the boil and cook for 8–10 minutes, until tender but still firm to the bite. Drain thoroughly, refresh in cold water and drain again. Toss the pasta in the oil.

Mix the lime juice, fish sauce and honey together in a small pan and cook over a medium heat for about 2 minutes.

Add the spring onions, cucumber, tomato wedges and mint to the pan, then add the steak and mix well. Season to taste with salt.

Transfer the pasta to a large, warmed serving dish and top with the steak and salad mixture. Serve just warm or leave to cool completely.

Spicy Sausage Pasta Salad

serves 4

125g/4½ oz dried conchiglie

2 tbsp olive oil

1 medium onion, chopped

2 garlic cloves, crushed

1 small yellow pepper, deseeded and cut into matchsticks

175 g/6 oz spicy pork sausage, such as chorizo, Italian pepperoni or salami, skinned and sliced

2 tbsp red wine

1 tbsp red wine vinegar

mixed salad leaves

salt

Bring a pan of lightly salted water to the boil over a medium heat. Add the pasta, bring back to the boil and cook for 8–10 minutes, or until tender but still firm to the bite.

Heat the oil in a pan over a medium heat. Add the onion and fry until translucent. Stir in the garlic, yellow pepper and sliced sausage and cook for about 3–4 minutes, stirring once or twice.

Add the wine, vinegar and reserved pasta to the pan, stir to blend well and bring the mixture just to the boil over a medium heat.

Arrange the salad leaves on 4 large serving plates, spoon over the warm sausage and pasta mixture and serve immediately.

Pasta Salad with Melon & Prawns

serves 6

225 g/8 oz dried green fusilli

5 tbsp extra virgin olive oil

450 g/1 lb cooked prawns

1 Charentais melon

1 Galia melon

1 tbsp red wine vinegar

1 tsp Dijon mustard

pinch of caster sugar

1 tbsp chopped fresh flat-leaf parsley

1 tbsp chopped fresh basil

1 oakleaf or quattro stagioni lettuce, shredded

salt and pepper

fresh basil leaves, to garnish

Bring a large pan of salted water to the boil. Add the pasta, bring back to the boil and cook for 8–10 minutes, or until tender but still firm to the bite. Drain, toss with 1 tablespoon of the olive oil and leave to cool.

Meanwhile, peel and devein the prawns, then place them in a large bowl. Halve both the melons and scoop out the seeds with a spoon. Using a melon baller or teaspoon, scoop out balls of the flesh and add them to the prawns.

Whisk together the remaining olive oil, the vinegar, mustard, sugar, parsley and chopped basil in a small bowl. Season to taste with salt and pepper. Add the cooled pasta to the prawn and melon mixture and toss lightly to mix, then pour in the dressing and toss again. Cover with clingfilm and chill in the refrigerator for 30 minutes.

Make a bed of shredded lettuce on a serving plate. Spoon the pasta salad on top, garnish with basil leaves and serve.

Neapolitan Seafood Salad

serves 4

450 g/1 lb prepared squid, cut into strips

750 g/1 lb 10 oz cooked mussels

450 g/1 lb cooked cockles in brine, drained

150 ml/5 fl oz white wine

300 ml/10 fl oz olive oil

225 g/8 oz dried orecchiette

juice of 1 lemon

1 bunch chives, snipped

1 bunch fresh parsley, finely chopped

mixed salad leaves

4 large tomatoes, quartered

salt and pepper

Put all of the seafood into a large bowl, pour over the wine and half of the olive oil, and set aside for 6 hours.

Put the seafood mixture into a saucepan and simmer over a low heat for 10 minutes. Set aside to cool.

Bring a large saucepan of lightly salted water to the boil. Add the pasta and 1 tbsp of the remaining olive oil and cook for 8–10 minutes, or until tender but still firm to the bite. Drain thoroughly and refresh in cold water.

Strain off about half of the cooking liquid from the seafood and discard the rest. Mix in the lemon juice, chives, parsley and the remaining olive oil. Season to taste with salt and pepper. Drain the pasta and add to the seafood.

Shred the salad leaves and arrange them in the base of a salad bowl. Spoon the seafood salad into the bowl, top with the tomatoes and serve.

Tuna & Herbed Fusilli Salad

serves 4

200 g/7 oz dried fusilli

1 red pepper, deseeded and quartered

1 red onion, sliced

4 tomatoes, sliced

200 g/7 oz canned tuna in brine, drained and flaked

for the dressing

6 tbsp basil-flavoured oil or extra virgin olive oil

3 tbsp white wine vinegar

1 tbsp lime juice

1 tsp mustard

1 tsp honey

4 tbsp chopped fresh basil, plus extra sprigs to garnish

Bring a large saucepan of lightly salted water to the boil. Add the pasta, return to the boil and cook for 8–10 minutes, or until tender but still firm to the bite.

Meanwhile, put the pepper quarters under a preheated hot grill and cook for 10–12 minutes until the skins begin to blacken. Transfer to a polythene bag, seal and set aside.

Remove the pasta from the heat, drain and set aside to cool. Remove the pepper quarters from the bag and peel off the skins. Slice the pepper into strips.

To make the dressing, put all the dressing ingredients in a large bowl and stir together well. Add the pasta, pepper strips, onion, tomatoes and tuna. Toss together gently, then divide between serving bowls. Garnish with sprigs of basil and serve.

Meat &
Poultry

Spaghetti Bolognese

serves 4

1 tbsp olive oil

1 onion, finely chopped

2 garlic cloves, chopped

1 carrot, chopped

1 celery stick, chopped

50 g/1¾ oz pancetta or streaky bacon, diced

350 g/12 oz fresh lean beef mince

400 g/14 oz canned chopped tomatoes

2 tsp dried oregano

125 ml/4 fl oz red wine

2 tbsp tomato purée

350 g/12 oz dried spaghetti

salt and pepper

chopped fresh parsley, to garnish

Heat the oil in a large frying pan. Add the onion and cook for 3 minutes. Add the garlic, carrot, celery and pancetta and cook for 3–4 minutes, or until just beginning to brown.

Add the beef and cook over a high heat for a further 3 minutes, or until the meat has browned. Stir in the tomatoes, oregano and red wine and bring to the boil. Reduce the heat and leave to simmer for about 45 minutes.

Stir in the tomato purée and season to taste with salt and pepper.

Cook the spaghetti in a pan of lightly salted boiling water for 8–10 minutes, or until tender but still firm to the bite. Drain thoroughly.

Transfer the spaghetti to a serving plate and pour over the bolognese sauce. Toss to mix well, garnish with parsley and serve hot.

Spaghetti with Meatballs

serves 6

1 potato, diced

400 g/14 oz fresh steak mince

1 onion, finely chopped

1 egg

4 tbsp chopped fresh flat-leaf parsley

plain flour, for dusting

5 tbsp olive oil

400 ml/14 fl oz passata

2 tbsp tomato purée

400 g/14 oz dried spaghetti

salt and pepper

fresh basil leaves and Parmesan cheese shavings, to garnish

Place the potato in a small saucepan, add cold water to cover and a pinch of salt and bring to the boil. Cook for 10–15 minutes until tender, then drain. Either mash thoroughly with a potato masher or fork or pass through a potato ricer.

Combine the potato, steak, onion, egg and parsley in a bowl and season to taste with salt and pepper. Spread out the flour on a plate. With dampened hands, shape the meat mixture into walnut-sized balls and roll in the flour. Shake off any excess.

Heat the oil in a heavy-based frying pan, add the meatballs and cook over a medium heat, stirring and turning frequently, for 8–10 minutes, or until golden all over.

Add the passata and tomato purée and cook for a further 10 minutes, or until the sauce is reduced and thickened.

Meanwhile, bring a large saucepan of lightly salted water to the boil. Add the pasta, return to the boil and cook for 8–10 minutes, or until tender but still firm to the bite.

Drain well and add to the meatball sauce, tossing well to coat. Transfer to a warmed serving dish, garnish with the basil leaves and Parmesan cheese shavings and serve immediately.

Spaghetti alla Carbonara

serves 4

450 g/1 lb dried spaghetti

1 tbsp olive oil

225 g/8 oz rindless pancetta or streaky bacon, chopped

4 eggs

5 tbsp single cream

2 tbsp freshly grated Parmesan cheese

salt and pepper

Bring a large, heavy-based saucepan of lightly salted water to the boil. Add the pasta, return to the boil and cook for 8–10 minutes, or until tender but still firm to the bite.

Meanwhile, heat the oil in a heavy-based frying pan. Add the pancetta and cook over a medium heat, stirring frequently, for 8–10 minutes.

Beat the eggs with the cream in a small bowl and season to taste with salt and pepper. Drain the pasta and return it to the saucepan. Tip in the contents of the frying pan, then add the egg mixture and half the Parmesan cheese. Stir well, then transfer to a warmed serving dish. Serve immediately, sprinkled with the remaining cheese.

Fusilli with Bacon, Eggs & Mushrooms

serves 6

1 tbsp olive oil

4 rashers streaky bacon or pancetta

115 g/4 oz mushrooms, sliced

225 g/8 oz dried fusilli

2 eggs, beaten

115 g/4 oz Cheddar or mozzarella cheese, cubed

salt and pepper

chopped fresh flat-leaf parsley, to garnish

Heat the oil in a frying pan over a medium heat. Add the bacon and fry until crisp. Remove with tongs, cut into small pieces and keep warm.

Fry the mushrooms in the pan with the bacon fat for 5–7 minutes until soft. Remove from the heat.

Cook the pasta in a pan of lightly salted boiling water for 8–10 minutes, or until tender but still firm to the bite.

Stir the mushrooms, beaten eggs and the cheese cubes into the pasta. Season with pepper and toss until the eggs have coated the pasta and the cheese has melted.

Transfer to a warm serving dish. Sprinkle with the bacon pieces and parsley and serve at once.

Pasta with Bacon & Tomatoes

serves 4

900 g/2 lb small, sweet tomatoes

6 rashers rindless smoked bacon

55 g/2 oz butter

1 onion, chopped

1 garlic clove, crushed

4 sprigs of fresh oregano, finely chopped

450 g/1 lb dried orecchiette

1 tbsp olive oil

salt and pepper

freshly grated pecorino cheese, to serve

Blanch the tomatoes in boiling water. Drain, skin and seed the tomatoes, then coarsely chop the flesh.

Using a sharp knife, chop the bacon into small dice. Melt the butter in a saucepan. Add the bacon and cook until it is golden.

Add the onion and garlic and cook over a medium heat for 5–7 minutes, until just softened.

Add the tomatoes and oregano to the saucepan and then season to taste with salt and pepper. Lower the heat and simmer for 10–12 minutes.

Bring a large pan of lightly salted water to the boil. Add the orecchiette and oil and cook for 8–10 minutes, or until just tender but still firm to the bite. Drain the pasta and transfer to a warmed serving dish or bowl.

Spoon the bacon and tomato sauce over the pasta, toss to coat and serve with the pecorino cheese.

Linguine with Bacon & Olives

serves 4

3 tbsp olive oil

2 onions, thinly sliced

2 garlic cloves, finely chopped

175 g/6 oz rindless lean bacon, diced

225 g/8 oz mushrooms, sliced

5 canned anchovy fillets, drained

6 black olives, stoned and halved

450 g/1 lb dried linguine

25 g/1 oz freshly grated Parmesan cheese

salt and pepper

Heat the olive oil in a large frying pan. Add the onions, garlic and bacon and cook over a low heat, stirring occasionally, until the onions are softened. Stir in the mushrooms, anchovies and olives, then season to taste with salt, if necessary, and pepper. Simmer for 5 minutes.

Meanwhile, bring a large, heavy-based saucepan of lightly salted water to the boil. Add the pasta, return to the boil and cook for 8–10 minutes, or until tender but still firm to the bite.

Drain the pasta and transfer to a warmed serving dish. Spoon the sauce on top, toss lightly and sprinkle with the Parmesan cheese. Serve immediately.

Farfalle with Gorgonzola & Ham

serves 4

225 ml/8 fl oz crème fraîche

225 g/8 oz chestnut mushrooms, quartered

400 g/14 oz dried farfalle

85 g/3 oz Gorgonzola cheese, crumbled

1 tbsp chopped fresh flat-leaf parsley, plus extra sprigs to garnish

175 g/6 oz cooked ham, diced

salt and pepper

Pour the crème fraîche into a saucepan, add the mushrooms and season to taste with salt and pepper. Bring to just below the boil, then lower the heat and simmer very gently, stirring occasionally, for 8–10 minutes, until the cream has thickened.

Meanwhile, bring a large pan of lightly salted water to the boil. Add the pasta, bring back to the boil and cook for 8–10 minutes, until tender but still firm to the bite.

Remove the pan of mushrooms from the heat and stir in the Gorgonzola cheese until it has melted. Return the pan to a very low heat and stir in the chopped parsley and ham.

Drain the pasta and add it to the sauce. Toss lightly, then divide among individual warmed plates, garnish with the sprigs of parsley and serve.

Penne with Ham, Tomato & Chilli

serves 4

1 tbsp olive oil

2 tbsp butter

1 onion, finely chopped

150 g/5½ oz ham, diced

2 garlic cloves, very finely chopped

1 fresh red chilli, seeded and finely chopped

800 g/1 lb 12 oz canned chopped tomatoes

450 g/1 lb dried penne

2 tbsp chopped fresh flat-leaf parsley

6 tbsp freshly grated Parmesan cheese

salt and pepper

Put the olive oil and 1 tablespoon of the butter in a large saucepan over a medium-low heat. Add the onion and fry for 10 minutes until soft and golden. Add the ham and fry for a further 5 minutes until lightly browned. Stir in the garlic, chilli and tomatoes. Season to taste with salt and pepper. Bring to the boil, then simmer over a medium-low heat for 30–40 minutes until thickened.

Cook the pasta in a pan of lightly salted boiling water for 8–10 minutes, or until tender but still firm to the bite. Drain and transfer to a warmed serving dish.

Pour the sauce over the pasta. Add the parsley, Parmesan cheese and the remaining butter. Toss well to mix and serve immediately.

Saffron Linguine

serves 4

350 g/12 oz dried linguine

pinch of saffron threads

2 tbsp water

140 g/5 oz ham, cut into strips

175 ml/6 fl oz double cream

55 g/2 oz freshly grated Parmesan cheese

2 egg yolks

salt and pepper

Bring a large, heavy-based saucepan of lightly salted water to the boil. Add the pasta, return to the boil and cook for 8–10 minutes, or until tender but still firm to the bite.

Meanwhile, place the saffron in a separate heavy-based saucepan and add the water. Bring to the boil, then remove from the heat and leave to stand for 5 minutes.

Stir the ham, cream and Parmesan cheese into the saffron and return the saucepan to the heat. Season to taste with salt and pepper and heat through gently, stirring constantly, until simmering. Remove the saucepan from the heat and beat in the egg yolks. Drain the pasta and transfer to a warmed serving dish. Add the saffron sauce, toss well and serve immediately.

Penne with Sausage Sauce

serves 4–6

2 tbsp olive oil

1 red onion, coarsely chopped

2 garlic cloves, coarsely chopped

6 Italian sausages, skinned and the meat crumbled

½ tsp dried chilli flakes

2 tbsp chopped fresh oregano

400 g/14 oz canned chopped tomatoes

350 g/12 oz dried penne

salt and pepper

2 tbsp chopped fresh flat-leaf parsley, to garnish

3 tbsp freshly grated Parmesan cheese, to serve

Heat the oil in a large saucepan, add the onion and cook over a medium heat, stirring frequently, for 6–8 minutes until starting to brown. Add the garlic and the crumbled sausages and cook for 8–10 minutes, breaking up the sausages with a wooden spoon.

Add the chilli flakes and oregano and stir well. Pour in the tomatoes and bring to the boil, then reduce the heat and simmer, uncovered, for 4–5 minutes until reduced and thickened. Season to taste with salt and pepper.

Meanwhile, bring a large saucepan of salted water to the boil. Add the pasta and stir well, return to the boil and cook for 8–10 minutes, or until tender but still firm to the bite. Drain well and return to the saucepan.

Pour the sauce into the pasta and stir well.

Transfer to warmed serving dishes, garnish with parsley and serve immediately with Parmesan cheese.

Pepperoni Pasta

serves 4

3 tbsp olive oil

1 onion, chopped

1 red pepper, deseeded and diced

1 orange pepper, deseeded and diced

800 g/1 lb 12 oz canned chopped tomatoes

1 tbsp sun-dried tomato paste

1 tsp paprika

225 g/8 oz pepperoni sausage, sliced

2 tbsp chopped fresh flat-leaf parsley, plus extra to garnish

450 g/1 lb dried penne

salt and pepper

Heat 2 tablespoons of the oil in a large, heavy-based frying pan. Add the onion and cook over a low heat, stirring occasionally, for 5 minutes, or until softened. Add the red and orange peppers, tomatoes and their can juices, sun-dried tomato paste and paprika and bring to the boil.

Add the pepperoni and parsley and season to taste with salt and pepper. Stir well, bring to the boil, then reduce the heat and simmer for 10–15 minutes.

Meanwhile, bring a large, heavy-based saucepan of lightly salted water to the boil. Add the pasta, return to the boil and cook for 8–10 minutes, or until tender but still firm to the bite. Drain well and transfer to a warmed serving dish. Add the remaining olive oil and toss. Add the sauce and toss again. Sprinkle with parsley and serve immediately.

Rigatoni with Chorizo & Mushrooms

serves 4

4 tbsp olive oil

1 red onion, chopped

1 garlic clove, chopped

1 celery stick, sliced

400 g/14 oz dried rigatoni

280 g/10 oz chorizo
sausage, sliced

225 g/8 oz chestnut
mushrooms, halved

1 tbsp chopped fresh
coriander

1 tbsp lime juice

salt and pepper

Heat the oil in a frying pan. Add the onion, garlic and celery and cook over a low heat, stirring occasionally, for 5 minutes, until softened.

Meanwhile, bring a large saucepan of lightly salted water to the boil. Add the pasta, bring back to the boil and cook for 8–10 minutes, or until tender but still firm to the bite.

While the pasta is cooking, add the chorizo to the frying pan and cook, stirring occasionally, for 5 minutes, until evenly browned. Add the mushrooms and cook, stirring occasionally, for a further 5 minutes. Stir in the coriander and lime juice and season to taste with salt and pepper.

Drain the pasta and return it to the pan. Add the chorizo and mushroom mixture and toss lightly. Divide among individual warmed plates and serve immediately.

Pasticcio

serves 4

1 tbsp olive oil

1 onion, chopped

2 garlic cloves, finely chopped

450 g/1 lb fresh lamb mince

2 tbsp tomato purée

2 tbsp plain flour

300 ml/10 fl oz chicken stock

1 tsp ground cinnamon

115 g/4 oz dried macaroni

2 beef tomatoes, sliced

300 ml/10 fl oz Greek yogurt

2 eggs, lightly beaten

salt and pepper

Preheat the oven to 190°C/375°F/Gas Mark 5. Heat the oil in a large, heavy-based frying pan. Add the onion and garlic and cook over a low heat, stirring occasionally, for 5 minutes, or until softened. Add the lamb and cook, breaking it up with a wooden spoon, until browned all over. Add the tomato purée and sprinkle in the flour. Cook, stirring, for 1 minute, then stir in the chicken stock. Season to taste with salt and pepper and stir in the cinnamon. Bring to the boil, reduce the heat, cover and cook for 25 minutes.

Meanwhile, bring a large, heavy-based saucepan of lightly salted water to the boil. Add the pasta, return to the boil and cook for 8–10 minutes, or until tender but still firm to the bite.

Drain the pasta and stir into the lamb mixture. Spoon into a large ovenproof dish and arrange the tomato slices on top. Beat together the yogurt and eggs then spoon over the lamb evenly. Bake in the preheated oven for 1 hour. Serve immediately.

Chicken with Creamy Penne

serves 2

200 g/7 oz dried penne

1 tbsp olive oil

2 skinless, boneless
chicken breasts

4 tbsp dry white wine

115 g/4 oz frozen peas

5 tbsp double cream

salt

4–5 tbsp chopped fresh
parsley, to garnish

Bring a large, heavy-based saucepan of lightly salted water to the boil. Add the pasta, return to the boil and cook for 8–10 minutes, or until tender but still firm to the bite.

Meanwhile, heat the oil in a frying pan, add the chicken breasts and cook over a medium heat for about 4 minutes on each side.

Pour in the wine and cook over a high heat until it has almost evaporated.

Drain the pasta. Add the peas, cream and pasta to the chicken breasts in the frying pan and stir well. Cover and simmer for 2 minutes. Serve immediately sprinkled with chopped parsley.

Spaghetti with Parsley Chicken

serves 4

1 tbsp olive oil

thinly pared rind of 1 lemon, cut into julienne strips

1 tsp finely chopped fresh root ginger

1 tsp sugar

225 ml/8 fl oz chicken stock

250 g/9 oz dried spaghetti

55 g/2 oz butter

225 g/8 oz skinless, boneless chicken breasts, diced

1 red onion, finely chopped

leaves from 2 bunches of fresh flat-leaf parsley

salt

Heat the oil in a heavy-based saucepan. Add the lemon rind and cook over a low heat, stirring frequently, for 5 minutes. Stir in the ginger and sugar, season to taste with salt and cook, stirring constantly, for a further 2 minutes. Pour in the chicken stock, bring to the boil, then cook for 5 minutes, or until the liquid has reduced by half.

Meanwhile, bring a large, heavy-based saucepan of lightly salted water to the boil. Add the pasta, return to the boil and cook for 8–10 minutes, or until tender but still firm to the bite.

Melt half the butter in a frying pan. Add the chicken and onion and cook, stirring frequently, for 5 minutes, or until the chicken is light brown all over. Stir in the lemon and ginger mixture and cook for 1 minute. Stir in the parsley leaves and cook, stirring constantly, for a further 3 minutes.

Drain the pasta and transfer to a warmed serving dish, then add the remaining butter and toss well. Add the chicken sauce, toss again and serve.

Penne with Chicken & Feta

serves 4

2 tbsp olive oil

450 g/1 lb skinless, boneless chicken breasts, cut into thin strips

6 spring onions, chopped

225 g/8 oz feta cheese, diced

4 tbsp snipped fresh chives

450 g/1 lb dried penne

salt and pepper

Heat the oil in a heavy-based frying pan. Add the chicken and cook over a medium heat, stirring frequently, for 5–8 minutes, or until golden all over and cooked through. Add the spring onions and cook for 2 minutes. Stir the feta cheese into the frying pan with half the chives and season to taste with salt and pepper.

Meanwhile, bring a large, heavy-based saucepan of lightly salted water to the boil. Add the pasta, return to the boil and cook for 8–10 minutes, or until tender but still firm to the bite. Drain well, then transfer to a warmed serving dish.

Spoon the chicken mixture onto the pasta, toss lightly and serve immediately, garnished with the remaining chives.

Farfalle with Chicken, Broccoli & Peppers

serves 4

4 tbsp olive oil

5 tbsp butter

3 garlic cloves, very finely chopped

450 g/1 lb skinless, boneless chicken breasts, diced

¼ tsp dried chilli flakes

450 g/1 lb small broccoli florets

300 g/10½ oz dried farfalle

175 g/6 oz bottled roasted red peppers, drained and diced

250 ml/9 fl oz chicken stock

salt and pepper

Bring a large pan of lightly salted water to the boil. Meanwhile, heat the oil and butter in a large frying pan over a medium-low heat. Cook the garlic until just beginning to colour.

Add the diced chicken, raise the heat to medium and cook for 4–5 minutes, until the chicken is no longer pink. Add the chilli flakes and season to taste with salt and pepper. Remove from the heat.

Plunge the broccoli into the boiling water and cook for 2 minutes until tender-crisp. Remove with a perforated spoon and set aside. Bring the water back to the boil. Add the pasta and cook for 8–10 minutes, or until tender but still firm to the bite. Drain and add to the chicken mixture in the pan. Add the broccoli and roasted peppers. Pour in the stock. Simmer briskly over a medium-high heat, stirring frequently, until most of the liquid has been absorbed.

Transfer to warmed dishes and serve.

Italian Chicken Spirals

serves 4

4 skinless, boneless chicken breasts

25 g/1 oz fresh basil leaves

15 g/½ oz hazelnuts

1 garlic clove, crushed

250 g/9 oz dried wholewheat fusilli

2 sun-dried tomatoes or fresh tomatoes

1 tbsp lemon juice

1 tbsp olive oil

1 tbsp capers

55 g/2 oz black olives

salt and pepper

Beat the chicken breasts with a rolling pin to flatten evenly.

Place the basil and hazelnuts in a food processor and process until finely chopped. Mix with the garlic and salt and pepper to taste.

Spread the basil mixture over the chicken breasts and roll up from one short end to enclose the filling. Wrap the chicken roll tightly in foil so that they hold their shape, then seal the ends well.

Bring a pan of lightly salted water to the boil and cook the pasta for 8–10 minutes, or until tender but still firm to the bite. Meanwhile, place the chicken parcels in a steamer or colander set over the pan, cover tightly, and steam for 10 minutes.

Using a sharp knife, dice the tomatoes.

Drain the pasta and return to the pan with the lemon juice, oil, tomatoes, capers and olives. Heat through.

Pierce the chicken with a skewer to make sure that the juices run clear and not pink. Slice the chicken, arrange over the pasta and serve.

Fish & Seafood

Spaghetti alla Puttanesca

serves 4

3 tbsp olive oil

2 garlic cloves, finely chopped

10 canned anchovy fillets, drained and chopped

140 g/5 oz black olives, stoned and chopped

1 tbsp capers, drained and rinsed

450 g/1 lb plum tomatoes, peeled, deseeded and chopped

pinch of cayenne pepper

400 g/14 oz dried spaghetti

salt

2 tbsp chopped fresh parsley, to garnish

Heat the oil in a heavy-based frying pan. Add the garlic and cook over a low heat, stirring frequently, for 2 minutes. Add the anchovies and mash them to a pulp with a fork. Add the olives, capers and tomatoes and season to taste with cayenne pepper. Cover and simmer for 25 minutes.

Meanwhile, bring a large, heavy-based saucepan of lightly salted water to the boil. Add the pasta, return to the boil and cook for 8–10 minutes, or until tender but still firm to the bite. Drain well and transfer to a warmed serving dish.

Spoon the anchovy sauce into the dish and toss the pasta, using 2 large forks. Garnish with the chopped parsley and serve immediately.

Penne with Sicilian Sauce

serves 4

50 g/1¾ oz sultanas

450 g/1 lb tomatoes, halved

25 g/1 oz pine kernels

50 g/1¾ oz canned anchovies, drained and halved lengthways

2 tbsp tomato purée

350 g/12 oz dried penne

Soak the sultanas in a bowl of warm water for about 20 minutes. Drain the sultanas thoroughly.

Preheat the grill, then cook the tomatoes under the hot grill for 10 minutes. Leave to cool slightly, then once cool enough to handle, peel off the skin and dice the flesh. Place the pine kernels on a baking tray and lightly toast under the grill for 2–3 minutes, or until golden brown.

Place the tomatoes, pine kernels and sultanas in a small saucepan and heat gently. Add the anchovies and tomato purée, and cook the sauce over a low heat for a further 2–3 minutes, or until hot.

Meanwhile, bring a large, heavy-based saucepan of lightly salted water to the boil. Add the pasta, return to the boil and cook for 8–10 minutes, or until tender but still firm to the bite. Drain thoroughly, then transfer the pasta to a serving plate and serve with the Sicilian sauce.

Fettuccine with Spinach & Anchovies

serves 4

900 g/2 lb fresh, young spinach leaves

400 g/14 oz dried fettuccine

5 tbsp olive oil

3 tbsp pine kernels

3 garlic cloves, crushed

8 canned anchovy fillets, drained and chopped

salt

Trim off any tough spinach stalks. Rinse the spinach leaves under cold running water and place them in a large saucepan with only the water that is clinging to them after washing. Cover and cook over a high heat, shaking the saucepan from time to time, until the spinach has wilted, but retains its colour. Drain well, reserve and keep warm.

Bring a large, heavy-based saucepan of lightly salted water to the boil. Add the fettuccine, return to the boil and cook for 8–10 minutes, or until tender but still firm to the bite.

Heat 4 tablespoons of the oil in a separate saucepan. Add the pine kernels and fry until golden. Remove the pine kernels from the saucepan and reserve until required.

Add the garlic to the saucepan and fry until golden. Add the anchovies and stir in the spinach. Cook, stirring, for 2–3 minutes, until heated through. Return the pine kernels to the saucepan.

Drain the fettuccine, toss in the remaining oil and transfer to a warmed serving dish. Spoon the anchovy and spinach sauce over the fettuccine, toss lightly and serve immediately.

Spaghetti with Tuna & Parsley

serves 6

500 g/1 lb 2 oz dried spaghetti

25 g/1 oz butter

200 g/7 oz canned tuna, drained

55 g/2 oz canned anchovies, drained

250 ml/9 fl oz olive oil

1 large bunch of fresh flat-leaf parsley, coarsely chopped, plus extra sprigs to garnish

150 ml/5 fl oz crème fraîche

salt and pepper

Bring a large, heavy-based saucepan of lightly salted water to the boil. Add the spaghetti, return to the boil and cook for 8–10 minutes, or until tender but still firm to the bite. Drain the spaghetti in a colander and return to the saucepan. Add the butter, toss thoroughly to coat and keep warm until required.

Flake the tuna into smaller pieces using 2 forks. Place the tuna in a food processor or blender with the anchovies, oil and parsley and process until the sauce is smooth. Pour in the crème fraîche and process for a few seconds to blend. Taste the sauce and season with salt and pepper, if necessary.

Shake the saucepan of spaghetti over a medium heat for a few minutes, or until it is thoroughly warmed.

Pour the sauce over the spaghetti and toss quickly, using 2 forks. Serve immediately, garnished with sprigs of parsley.

Spaghettini with Quick Tuna Sauce

serves 4

3 tbsp olive oil

4 tomatoes, peeled, deseeded and coarsely chopped

115 g/4 oz mushrooms, sliced

1 tbsp shredded fresh basil

400 g/14 oz canned tuna, drained

100 ml/3½ fl oz fish stock or chicken stock

1 garlic clove, finely chopped

2 tsp chopped fresh marjoram

350 g/12 oz dried spaghettini

salt and pepper

115 g/4 oz freshly grated Parmesan cheese, to serve

Heat the oil in a large frying pan. Add the tomatoes and cook over a low heat, stirring occasionally, for 15 minutes, or until pulpy. Add the mushrooms and cook, stirring occasionally, for a further 10 minutes. Stir in the basil, tuna, stock, garlic and marjoram and season to taste with salt and pepper. Cook over a low heat for 5 minutes, or until heated through.

Meanwhile, bring a large, heavy-based saucepan of lightly salted water to the boil. Add the pasta, return to the boil and cook for 8–10 minutes, or until tender but still firm to the bite.

Drain the pasta well, transfer to a warmed serving dish and spoon on the tuna mixture. Serve with grated Parmesan cheese.

Baked Tuna & Ricotta Rigatoni

serves 4

butter, for greasing

450 g/1 lb dried rigatoni

200 g/7 oz canned flaked tuna, drained

225 g/8 oz ricotta cheese

125 ml/4 fl oz double cream

225 g/8 oz freshly grated Parmesan cheese

115 g/4 oz sun-dried tomatoes, drained and sliced

salt and pepper

Preheat the oven to 200°C/400°F/Gas Mark 6. Lightly grease a large ovenproof dish with butter. Bring a large, heavy-based saucepan of lightly salted water to the boil. Add the rigatoni, return to the boil and cook for 8–10 minutes, or until tender but still firm to the bite. Drain the pasta and leave until cool enough to handle.

Meanwhile, mix the tuna and ricotta cheese together in a bowl to form a soft paste. Spoon the mixture into a piping bag and use to fill the rigatoni. Arrange the filled pasta tubes side by side in the prepared dish.

To make the sauce, mix the cream and Parmesan cheese together in a bowl and season to taste with salt and pepper. Spoon the sauce over the rigatoni and top with the sun-dried tomatoes, arranged in a criss-cross pattern. Bake in the preheated oven for 20 minutes. Serve hot straight from the dish.

Tagliatelle with Smoked Salmon & Rocket

serves 4

350 g/12 oz dried tagliatelle

2 tbsp olive oil

1 garlic clove, finely chopped

115 g/4 oz smoked salmon, cut into thin strips

55 g/2 oz rocket

salt and pepper

Bring a large, heavy-based saucepan of lightly salted water to the boil. Add the pasta, return to the boil and cook for 8–10 minutes, or until tender but still firm to the bite.

Just before the end of the cooking time, heat the olive oil in a heavy-based frying pan. Add the garlic and cook over a low heat, stirring constantly, for 1 minute. Do not allow the garlic to brown or it will taste bitter.

Add the salmon and rocket. Season to taste with pepper and cook, stirring constantly, for 1 minute. Remove the frying pan from the heat.

Drain the pasta and transfer to a warmed serving dish. Add the smoked salmon and rocket mixture, toss lightly and serve.

Conchiglie with Smoked Salmon & Soured Cream

serves 4

450 g/1 lb dried conchiglie

300 ml/10 fl oz soured cream

2 tsp Dijon mustard

4 large spring onions, sliced finely

225 g/8 oz smoked salmon, cut into bite-sized pieces

finely grated rind of ½ lemon

salt and pepper

2 tbsp snipped fresh chives, to garnish

Bring a large, heavy-based saucepan of lightly salted water to the boil. Add the pasta, return to the boil and cook for 8–10 minutes, or until tender but still firm to the bite. Drain and return to the pan.

Add the soured cream, mustard, spring onions, smoked salmon and lemon rind to the pasta. Stir over a low heat until heated through. Season to taste with pepper.

Transfer to a serving dish and garnish with the chives. Serve warm or at room temperature.

Fusilli with Monkfish & Broccoli

serves 4

115 g/4 oz broccoli, separated into florets

3 tbsp olive oil

350 g/12 oz monkfish fillet, skinned and cut into bite-sized pieces

2 garlic cloves, crushed

125 ml/4 fl oz dry white wine

225 ml/8 fl oz double cream

400 g/14 oz dried fusilli

85 g/3 oz Gorgonzola cheese, diced

salt and pepper

Separate the broccoli florets into tiny sprigs. Bring a saucepan of lightly salted water to the boil, add the broccoli and cook for 2 minutes. Drain and refresh under cold running water.

Heat the oil in a large, heavy-based frying pan. Add the monkfish and garlic and season to taste with salt and pepper. Cook, stirring frequently, for 5 minutes, or until the fish is opaque. Pour in the white wine and cream and cook, stirring occasionally, for 5 minutes, or until the fish is cooked through and the sauce has thickened. Stir in the broccoli florets.

Meanwhile, bring a large, heavy-based saucepan of lightly salted water to the boil. Add the pasta, return to the boil and cook for 8–10 minutes, or until tender but still firm to the bite. Drain and tip the pasta into the saucepan with the fish, add the cheese and toss lightly. Serve immediately.

Sea Bass with Olive Sauce

serves 4

450 g/1 lb dried rigatoni

1 tbsp olive oil

8 x 115 g/4 oz sea bass fillets

salt

shredded leek and shredded carrot, to garnish

for the sauce

25 g/1 oz butter

4 shallots, chopped

2 tbsp capers

175 g/6 oz stoned green olives, chopped

4 tbsp balsamic vinegar

300 ml/10 fl oz fish stock

300 ml/10 fl oz double cream

juice of 1 lemon

salt and pepper

To make the sauce, melt the butter in a frying pan. Add the shallots and cook over a low heat for 4 minutes. Add the capers and olives and cook for a further 3 minutes.

Stir in the balsamic vinegar and fish stock, bring to the boil and reduce by half. Add the cream, stirring, and reduce again by half. Season to taste with salt and pepper and stir in the lemon juice. Remove the pan from the heat, set aside and keep warm.

Bring a large pan of lightly salted water to the boil. Add the pasta and olive oil and cook for 8–10 minutes, or until tender but still firm to the bite.

Meanwhile, lightly grill the sea bass fillets for 3–4 minutes on each side, until cooked through, but still moist and delicate.

Drain the pasta thoroughly and transfer to large individual serving dishes. Top the pasta with the fish and pour over the olive sauce. Garnish with shredded leek and shredded carrot and serve immediately.

Tagliatelle with Creamy Prawns

serves 4

3 tbsp olive oil

3 tbsp butter

4 garlic cloves, very finely chopped

2 tbsp finely diced red pepper

2 tbsp tomato purée

125 ml/4 fl oz dry white wine

450 g/1 lb dried tagliatelle

350 g/12 oz raw peeled prawns

125 ml/4 fl oz double cream

salt and pepper

3 tbsp chopped fresh flat-leaf parsley, to garnish

Heat the oil and butter in a saucepan over a medium-low heat. Add the garlic and red pepper. Cook for a few seconds until the garlic is just beginning to colour. Stir in the tomato purée and wine. Cook for 10 minutes, stirring.

Bring a large saucepan of lightly salted water to the boil. Add the pasta, bring back to the boil and cook for 8–10 minutes, or until tender but still firm to the bite. Drain and return to the pan.

Add the prawns to the sauce and raise the heat to medium-high. Cook for 2 minutes, stirring, until the prawns turn pink. Reduce the heat and stir in the cream. Cook for 1 minute, stirring constantly, until thickened. Season to taste with salt and pepper.

Transfer the pasta to a warmed serving dish. Pour the sauce over the pasta. Sprinkle with the parsley. Toss well to mix and serve immediately.

Fusilli with Prawns & Peas

serves 4

pinch of saffron threads

225 ml/8 fl oz dry white
wine

3 tbsp olive oil

25 g/1 oz unsalted butter

1 shallot, chopped

225 g/8 oz peas

350 g/12 oz cooked peeled
prawns

350 g/12 oz dried fusilli

salt and pepper

2 tbsp snipped fresh dill,
to garnish

Place the saffron in a small bowl, add the wine and leave to soak. Heat the olive oil and butter in a large, heavy-based frying pan. Add the shallot and cook over a low heat, stirring occasionally, for 5 minutes, or until softened. Add the peas and prawns and cook, stirring occasionally, for 2–3 minutes.

Bring a large, heavy-based saucepan of lightly salted water to the boil. Add the pasta, return to the boil and cook for 8–10 minutes, or until tender but still firm to the bite.

Meanwhile, stir the saffron and wine mixture into the frying pan. Increase the heat and cook until the liquid is reduced by about half. Season to taste with salt and pepper. Drain the pasta and add to the frying pan. Cook for 1–2 minutes, or until it is well coated with the sauce. Transfer to a warmed serving dish, sprinkle with dill and serve immediately.

Tagliatelle with Prawns & Scallops

serves 6

450 g/1 lb raw prawns

25 g/1 oz butter

2 shallots, finely chopped

225 ml/8 fl oz dry white vermouth

350 ml/12 fl oz water

450 g/1 lb dried tagliatelle

2 tbsp olive oil

450 g/1 lb prepared scallops

2 tbsp snipped fresh chives

salt and pepper

Peel and devein the prawns, reserving the shells. Melt the butter in a heavy-based frying pan. Add the shallots and cook over a low heat, stirring occasionally, for 5 minutes, or until softened. Add the prawn shells and cook, stirring constantly, for 1 minute. Pour in the vermouth and cook, stirring, for 1 minute. Add the water, bring to the boil, then reduce the heat and simmer for 10 minutes, or until the liquid has reduced by half. Remove the frying pan from the heat.

Bring a large, heavy-based saucepan of lightly salted water to the boil. Add the pasta, return to the boil and cook for 8–10 minutes, or until tender but still firm to the bite.

Meanwhile, heat the olive oil in a separate heavy-based frying pan. Add the scallops and prawns and cook, stirring frequently, for 2 minutes, or until the scallops are opaque and the prawns have changed colour. Strain the prawn-shell stock into the frying pan. Drain the pasta and add to the frying pan with the chives and season to taste with salt and pepper. Toss well over a low heat for 1 minute, then serve.

Pappardelle with Scallops & Porcini

serves 4

25 g/1 oz dried porcini mushrooms

500 ml/18 fl oz hot water

3 tbsp olive oil

3 tbsp butter

350 g/12 oz prepared scallops, sliced

2 garlic cloves, very finely chopped

2 tbsp lemon juice

250 ml/9 fl oz double cream

350 g/12 oz dried pappardelle

salt and pepper

2 tbsp chopped fresh flat-leaf parsley, to garnish

Put the porcini and hot water in a bowl. Leave to soak for 20 minutes. Strain the mushrooms, reserving the soaking water, and coarsely chop. Line a sieve with two pieces of kitchen paper and strain the mushroom water into a bowl.

Heat the oil and butter in a large frying pan over a medium heat. Add the scallops and cook for 2 minutes until just golden. Add the garlic and mushrooms, then cook for another minute.

Stir in the lemon juice, cream and 125 ml/4 fl oz of the mushroom water. Bring to the boil, then simmer over a medium heat for 2–3 minutes, stirring constantly, until the liquid is reduced by half. Season to taste with salt and pepper. Remove from the heat.

Meanwhile, bring a large saucepan of lightly salted water to the boil. Add the pasta, bring back to the boil and cook for 8–10 minutes, or until tender but still firm to the bite. Drain and transfer to a warmed serving dish. Briefly reheat the sauce and pour over the pasta. Sprinkle with the parsley and toss well to mix. Serve immediately.

Macaroni with Scallops & Pine Kernels

serves 4

400 g/14 oz dried long macaroni

4 tbsp olive oil

1 garlic clove, finely chopped

55 g/2 oz pine kernels

8 large prepared scallops, sliced

salt and pepper

2 tbsp shredded fresh basil leaves, to garnish

Bring a large, heavy-based saucepan of lightly salted water to the boil. Add the pasta, return to the boil and cook for 8–10 minutes, or until tender but still firm to the bite.

About 5 minutes before the pasta is ready, heat the oil in a frying pan. Add the garlic and cook for 1–2 minutes until softened but not browned. Add the pine kernels and cook until browned. Stir in the scallops and cook until just opaque. Season to taste with salt and pepper.

When the pasta is cooked, drain and return to the saucepan. Add the scallops, pine kernels, garlic and the juices in the frying pan to the pasta and toss together. Serve garnished with the shredded basil leaves.

Spaghetti Con Vongole

serves 4

1 kg/2 lb 4 oz live clams, scrubbed

175 ml/6 fl oz water

175 ml/6 fl oz dry white wine

350 g/12 oz dried spaghetti

5 tbsp olive oil

2 garlic cloves, finely chopped

4 tbsp chopped fresh flat-leaf parsley

salt and pepper

Discard any clams with broken shells or any that refuse to close when tapped. Place the clams in a large, heavy-based saucepan. Add the water and wine, then cover and cook over a high heat, shaking the saucepan occasionally, for 5 minutes, or until the shells have opened. Remove the clams with a slotted spoon and strain the liquid through a muslin-lined sieve into a small saucepan. Bring to the boil and cook until reduced by about half. Discard any clams that remain closed and remove the remainder from their shells.

Bring a large, heavy-based saucepan of lightly salted water to the boil. Add the pasta, return to the boil and cook for 8–10 minutes, or until tender but still firm to the bite.

Meanwhile, heat the oil in a large, heavy-based frying pan. Add the garlic and cook, stirring frequently, for 2 minutes. Add the parsley and the reduced cooking liquid and simmer gently. Drain the pasta and add it to the frying pan with the clams. Season to taste with salt and pepper and cook, stirring constantly, for 4 minutes, or until the pasta is coated and the clams have heated through. Transfer to a warmed serving dish and serve immediately.

Spaghetti with Crab

serves 4

1 dressed crab, about 450 g/
1 lb including the shell

350 g/12 oz dried spaghetti

6 tbsp extra virgin olive oil

1 fresh red chilli, deseeded
and finely chopped

2 garlic cloves, finely
chopped

3 tbsp chopped fresh
parsley

2 tbsp lemon juice

1 tsp finely grated lemon
rind

salt and pepper

lemon wedges, to garnish

Using a sharp knife, scoop the meat from the crab shell into a bowl. Mix the white and brown meat together lightly and reserve.

Bring a large pan of lightly salted water to the boil over a medium heat. Add the pasta and cook for 8–10 minutes, or until tender but still firm to the bite. Drain thoroughly and return to the pan.

Meanwhile, heat 2 tablespoons of the oil in a frying pan over a low heat. Add the chilli and garlic and cook for 30 seconds, then add the crabmeat, parsley, lemon juice and rind. Cook for 1 minute, until the crab is just heated through.

Add the crab mixture to the pasta with the remaining oil and season to taste with salt and pepper. Toss together thoroughly and transfer to a large, warmed serving dish and garnish with a few lemon wedges. Serve immediately.

Penne with Squid & Tomatoes

serves 4

225 g/8 oz dried penne

350 g/12 oz prepared squid

6 tbsp olive oil

2 onions, sliced

225 ml/8 fl oz fish stock or chicken stock

150 ml/5 fl oz full-bodied red wine

400 g/14 oz canned chopped tomatoes

2 tbsp tomato purée

1 tbsp chopped fresh marjoram

1 bay leaf

salt and pepper

2 tbsp chopped fresh parsley, to garnish

Bring a large, heavy-based saucepan of lightly salted water to the boil. Add the pasta, return to the boil and cook for 3 minutes, then drain and reserve until required. With a sharp knife, cut the squid into strips.

Heat the olive oil in a large saucepan. Add the onions and cook over a low heat, stirring occasionally, for 5 minutes, or until softened. Add the squid and stock, bring to the boil and simmer for 3 minutes. Stir in the wine, chopped tomatoes and their can juices, tomato purée, marjoram and bay leaf. Season to taste with salt and pepper. Bring to the boil and cook for 5 minutes, or until slightly reduced.

Add the pasta, return to the boil and simmer for 8–10 minutes, or until tender but still firm to the bite. Remove and discard the bay leaf. Transfer to a warmed serving dish, garnish with the parsley and serve immediately.

4

Vegetarian

Spaghetti with Tomatoes & Basil

serves 4

5 tbsp extra virgin olive oil

1 onion, finely chopped

800 g/1 lb 12 oz canned chopped tomatoes

4 garlic cloves, quartered

450 g/1 lb dried spaghetti

large handful fresh basil leaves, shredded

salt and pepper

freshly grated Parmesan cheese, to serve

Heat the oil in a large saucepan over a medium heat. Add the onion and cook gently for 5 minutes until soft. Add the tomatoes and garlic. Bring to the boil, then simmer over a medium-low heat for 25–30 minutes until the oil separates from the tomato. Season to taste with salt and pepper.

Bring a large, heavy-based saucepan of lightly salted water to the boil. Add the pasta, return to the boil and cook for 8–10 minutes, or until tender but still firm to the bite. Drain and transfer to a warmed serving dish.

Pour the sauce over the pasta. Add the basil and toss well to mix. Serve with Parmesan cheese.

Tagliatelle with Pesto

serves 4

450 g/1 lb dried tagliatelle

salt

sprigs of fresh basil,
to garnish

for the pesto

2 garlic cloves

25 g/1 oz pine kernels

115 g/4 oz fresh basil leaves

125 ml/4 fl oz olive oil

55 g/2 oz freshly grated
Parmesan cheese

salt

To make the pesto, put the garlic, pine kernels and a large pinch of salt into a blender or food processor and process briefly. Add the basil leaves and process to a paste. With the motor still running, gradually add the oil. Scrape into a bowl and beat in the Parmesan cheese. Season to taste with salt.

Bring a large saucepan of lightly salted water to the boil. Add the pasta, return to the boil and cook for 8–10 minutes, or until tender but still firm to the bite. Drain well, return to the saucepan and toss with half the pesto, then divide between warmed serving dishes and top with the remaining pesto. Garnish with sprigs of basil and serve.

Spaghetti Olio e Aglio

serves 4

450 g/1 lb dried spaghetti

125 ml/4 fl oz extra virgin olive oil

3 garlic cloves, finely chopped

3 tbsp chopped fresh flat-leaf parsley

salt and pepper

Bring a large, heavy-based saucepan of lightly salted water to the boil. Add the pasta, return to the boil and cook for 8–10 minutes, or until tender but still firm to the bite.

Meanwhile, heat the oil in a heavy-based frying pan. Add the garlic and a pinch of salt and cook over a low heat, stirring constantly, for 3–4 minutes, or until golden. Do not allow the garlic to brown or it will taste bitter. Remove the frying pan from the heat.

Drain the pasta and transfer to a warmed serving dish. Pour in the garlic-flavoured olive oil, then add the chopped parsley and season to taste with salt and pepper. Toss well and serve immediately.

Fettuccine with Garlic, Tomatoes & Olives

serves 4

4 plum tomatoes, peeled, deseeded and chopped

4 garlic cloves, finely chopped

8 black olives, stoned and finely chopped

1 fresh red chilli, deseeded and finely chopped

2 tbsp chopped fresh flat-leaf parsley

2 tbsp extra virgin olive oil

1 tbsp lemon juice

280 g/10 oz dried fettuccine

salt and pepper

Place the tomatoes in a large, non-metallic sieve set over a bowl. Cover and set aside in the refrigerator for 30 minutes.

Combine the garlic, olives, chilli, parsley, oil and lemon juice in a separate bowl. Season to taste with salt and pepper. Cover and set aside in the refrigerator until required.

Add the tomatoes to the garlic mixture, discarding the drained juice.

Bring a large saucepan of lightly salted water to the boil. Add the fettuccine, return to the boil and cook for 8–10 minutes, or until tender but still firm to the bite. Drain, then tip into a serving bowl. Add the garlic and tomato mixture and toss well. Serve immediately.

Creamy Pappardelle & Broccoli

serves 4

55 g/2 oz butter

1 large onion, finely chopped

450 g/1 lb broccoli, broken into florets

450 g/1 lb dried pappardelle

150 ml/5 fl oz vegetable stock

1 tbsp plain flour

150 ml/5 fl oz single cream

55 g/2 oz freshly grated mozzarella cheese

freshly grated nutmeg

salt and white pepper

fresh apple slices, to garnish

Melt half the butter in a large pan over a medium heat. Add the onion and fry for 4 minutes.

Add the broccoli and pasta to the pan and cook, stirring constantly, for 2 minutes. Add the stock, bring back to the boil and simmer for a further 8–10 minutes. Season well with salt and white pepper.

Meanwhile, melt the remaining butter in a pan over a medium heat. Sprinkle over the flour and cook, stirring constantly, for 2 minutes. Gradually stir in the cream and bring to simmering point, but do not boil. Add the mozzarella cheese and season to taste with salt and a little freshly grated nutmeg.

Drain the pasta and broccoli mixture and return to the pan. Pour over the cheese sauce. Cook, stirring occasionally, for 2 minutes. Transfer the pasta and broccoli mixture to warmed serving dishes and garnish with a few slices of fresh apple. Serve immediately.

Penne with Asparagus & Gorgonzola

serves 4

450 g/1 lb asparagus tips

olive oil

225 g/8 oz Gorgonzola cheese, crumbled

175 ml/6 fl oz double cream

350 g/12 oz dried penne

salt and pepper

Preheat the oven to 230°C/450°F/Gas Mark 8. Place the asparagus tips in a single layer in a shallow ovenproof dish. Sprinkle with a little olive oil. Season to taste with salt and pepper. Turn to coat in the oil and seasoning.

Roast in the preheated oven for 10–12 minutes until slightly browned and just tender. Set aside and keep warm.

Combine the crumbled cheese with the cream in a bowl. Season to taste with salt and pepper.

Bring a large, heavy-based saucepan of lightly salted water to the boil. Add the pasta, return to the boil and cook for 8–10 minutes, or until tender but still firm to the bite. Drain and transfer to a warmed serving dish.

Immediately add the asparagus and the cheese mixture to the pasta. Toss well until the cheese has melted and the pasta is coated with the sauce. Serve immediately.

Fusilli with Ricotta, Mint & Garlic

serves 4

300 g/10½ oz dried fusilli

140 g/5 oz ricotta cheese

1–2 roasted garlic cloves
from a jar, finely chopped

150 ml/5 fl oz double cream

1 tbsp chopped fresh mint,
plus extra sprigs
to garnish

salt and pepper

Bring a large, heavy-based saucepan of lightly salted water to the boil. Add the pasta, return to the boil and cook for 8–10 minutes, or until tender but still firm to the bite.

Beat the ricotta, garlic, cream and chopped mint together in a bowl until smooth.

Drain the cooked pasta then tip back into the pan. Pour in the cheese mixture and toss together.

Season to taste with pepper and serve immediately, garnished with the sprigs of mint.

Rigatoni with Peppers & Goat's Cheese

serves 4

2 tbsp olive oil

1 tbsp butter

1 small onion, finely chopped

4 peppers, yellow and red, deseeded and cut into 2-cm/¾-inch squares

3 garlic cloves, thinly sliced

450 g/1 lb dried rigatoni

125 g/4½ oz goat's cheese, crumbled

15 fresh basil leaves, shredded

10 black olives, stoned and sliced

salt and pepper

Heat the oil and butter in a large frying pan over a medium heat. Add the onion and cook until soft. Raise the heat to medium-high and add the peppers and garlic. Cook for 12–15 minutes, stirring, until the peppers are tender but not mushy. Season to taste with salt and pepper. Remove from the heat.

Bring a large saucepan of lightly salted water to the boil. Add the pasta, bring back to the boil and cook for 8–10 minutes, or until tender but still firm to the bite. Drain and transfer to a warmed serving dish. Add the goat's cheese and toss to mix.

Briefly reheat the onion and pepper mixture. Add the basil and olives. Pour over the pasta and toss well to mix. Serve immediately.

Tagliatelle with Wild Mushrooms & Mascarpone

serves 4

450 g/1 lb dried tagliatelle

55 g/2 oz butter

1 garlic clove, crushed

225 g/8 oz mixed wild mushrooms, sliced

250 g/9 oz mascarpone cheese

2 tbsp milk

1 tsp chopped fresh sage, plus extra leaves to garnish

salt and pepper

freshly grated Parmesan cheese, to serve

Bring a large, heavy-based saucepan of lightly salted water to the boil. Add the pasta, return to the boil and cook for 8–10 minutes, or until tender but still firm to the bite.

Meanwhile, melt the butter in a separate large saucepan. Add the garlic and mushrooms and cook for 3–4 minutes.

Reduce the heat and stir in the mascarpone cheese, milk and sage. Season to taste with salt and pepper.

Drain the pasta thoroughly and add to the mushroom sauce. Toss until the pasta is well coated with the sauce. Transfer to warmed serving dishes, garnish with sage leaves and serve immediately with Parmesan cheese.

Spaghetti alla Norma

serves 4

175 ml/6 fl oz olive oil

500 g/1 lb 2 oz plum tomatoes, peeled and chopped

1 garlic clove, chopped

350 g/12 oz aubergines, diced

400 g/14 oz dried spaghetti

½ bunch fresh basil, torn

115 g/4 oz freshly grated pecorino cheese

salt and pepper

Heat 4 tablespoons of the oil in a large saucepan. Add the tomatoes and garlic, season to taste with salt and pepper, cover and cook over a low heat, stirring occasionally, for 25 minutes.

Meanwhile, heat the remaining oil in a heavy-based frying pan. Add the aubergines and cook, stirring occasionally, for 5 minutes, until evenly golden brown. Remove with a perforated spoon and drain on kitchen paper.

Bring a large pan of salted water to the boil. Add the pasta, bring back to the boil and cook for 8–10 minutes, until tender but still firm to the bite.

Meanwhile, stir the drained aubergines into the pan of tomatoes. Taste and adjust the seasoning, if necessary.

Drain the pasta and place in a warmed serving dish. Add the tomato and aubergine mixture, basil and half the pecorino cheese. Toss well, sprinkle with the remaining pecorino cheese and serve immediately.

Fusilli with Courgettes & Lemon

serves 4

6 tbsp olive oil

1 small onion, very thinly sliced

2 garlic cloves, very finely chopped

2 tbsp chopped fresh rosemary

1 tbsp chopped fresh flat-leaf parsley

450 g/1 lb small courgettes, cut into 4-cm/1½-inch strips

finely grated rind of 1 lemon

450 g/1 lb dried fusilli

salt and pepper

4 tbsp freshly grated Parmesan cheese, to serve

Heat the oil in a large frying pan over a medium-low heat. Add the onion and cook gently, stirring occasionally, for about 10 minutes, until golden.

Raise the heat to medium-high. Add the garlic, rosemary and parsley. Cook for a few seconds, stirring.

Add the courgettes and lemon rind. Cook for 5–7 minutes, stirring occasionally, until the courgettes are just tender. Season to taste with salt and pepper. Remove from the heat.

Bring a large saucepan of lightly salted water to the boil. Add the pasta, bring back to the boil and cook for 8–10 minutes, or until tender but still firm to the bite. Drain and transfer to a warmed serving dish.

Briefly reheat the courgette sauce. Pour over the pasta and toss well to mix. Sprinkle with the Parmesan cheese and serve immediately.

Fusilli with Sun-dried Tomatoes

serves 4

85 g/3 oz sun-dried tomatoes (not in oil)

700 ml/1¼ pints boiling water

2 tbsp olive oil

1 onion, finely chopped

2 large garlic cloves, finely sliced

2 tbsp chopped fresh flat-leaf parsley

2 tsp chopped fresh oregano

1 tsp chopped fresh rosemary

350 g/12 oz dried fusilli

10 fresh basil leaves, shredded

salt and pepper

3 tbsp freshly grated Parmesan cheese, to serve

Put the tomatoes and boiling water in a bowl and leave to stand for 5 minutes. Using a perforated spoon, remove one-third of the tomatoes from the bowl. Cut into bite-sized pieces. Put the remaining tomatoes and water into a blender and purée.

Heat the oil in a large frying pan over a medium heat. Add the onion and cook gently for 5 minutes until soft. Add the garlic and cook until just beginning to colour. Add the puréed tomato and the reserved tomato pieces to the pan. Bring to the boil, then simmer over a medium-low heat for 10 minutes. Stir in the parsley, oregano and rosemary and season to taste with salt and pepper. Simmer for 1 minute, then remove from the heat.

Bring a large, heavy-based saucepan of lightly salted water to the boil. Add the pasta, return to the boil and cook for 8–10 minutes, or until tender but still firm to the bite. Drain and transfer to a warmed serving dish. Briefly reheat the sauce. Pour over the pasta, add the basil and toss well to mix. Sprinkle with the Parmesan cheese and serve immediately.

Tagliatelle with Walnuts

serves 4

25 g/1 oz fresh white breadcrumbs

350 g/12 oz walnut pieces

2 garlic cloves, finely chopped

4 tbsp milk

4 tbsp olive oil

85 g/3 oz fromage frais or cream cheese

150 ml/5 fl oz single cream

350 g/12 oz dried tagliatelle

salt and pepper

sprigs of fresh parsley, to garnish

Place the breadcrumbs, walnuts, garlic, milk, oil and fromage frais in a large mortar and grind to a smooth paste. Alternatively, place the ingredients in a food processor and process until smooth. Stir in the cream to give a thick sauce consistency and season to taste with salt and pepper. Reserve.

Bring a large, heavy-based saucepan of lightly salted water to the boil. Add the pasta, return to the boil and cook for 8–10 minutes, or until tender but still firm to the bite.

Drain the pasta and transfer to a warmed serving dish. Add the walnut sauce and toss thoroughly to coat. Garnish with parsley and serve immediately.

Pappardelle with Pumpkin Sauce

serves 4

55 g/2 oz butter

6 shallots, very finely chopped

800 g/1 lb 12 oz pumpkin, peeled, deseeded and cut into pieces

pinch of freshly grated nutmeg

200 ml/7 fl oz single cream

4 tbsp freshly grated Parmesan cheese, plus extra to serve

2 tbsp chopped fresh flat-leaf parsley

350 g/12 oz dried pappardelle

salt

Melt the butter in a large, heavy-based saucepan. Add the shallots, sprinkle with a little salt, cover and cook over a very low heat, stirring occasionally, for 30 minutes.

Add the pumpkin pieces and season to taste with nutmeg. Cover and cook over a very low heat, stirring occasionally, for 40 minutes, or until the pumpkin is pulpy. Stir in the cream, Parmesan cheese and parsley and remove the saucepan from the heat.

Meanwhile, bring a large, heavy-based saucepan of lightly salted water to the boil. Add the pasta, return to the boil and cook for 8–10 minutes, or until tender but still firm to the bite. Drain, reserving 2–3 tablespoons of the cooking water.

Add the pasta to the pumpkin mixture and stir in the reserved cooking water if the mixture seems too thick. Cook, stirring, for 1 minute, then transfer to a warmed serving dish and serve immediately with extra grated Parmesan cheese.

Tagliatelle with Garlic Crumbs

serves 4

350 g/12 oz fresh white breadcrumbs

4 tbsp finely chopped fresh flat-leaf parsley

1 tbsp snipped fresh chives

2 tbsp finely chopped fresh marjoram

3 tbsp olive oil, plus extra to serve

3–4 garlic cloves, finely chopped

55 g/2 oz pine kernels

450 g/1 lb dried green tagliatelle

salt and pepper

55 g/2 oz freshly grated pecorino cheese, to serve

Mix the breadcrumbs, parsley, chives and marjoram together in a small bowl. Heat the oil in a large, heavy-based frying pan. Add the breadcrumb mixture and the garlic and pine kernels, season to taste with salt and pepper and cook over a low heat, stirring constantly, for 5 minutes, or until the breadcrumbs become golden, but not crisp. Remove the frying pan from the heat and cover to keep warm.

Bring a large, heavy-based saucepan of lightly salted water to the boil. Add the pasta, return to the boil and cook for 8–10 minutes, or until tender but still firm to the bite.

Drain the pasta and transfer to a warmed serving dish. Drizzle with oil to taste and toss to mix. Add the garlic breadcrumbs and toss again. Serve immediately with the pecorino cheese.

Tagliatelle with Roasted Garlic & Red Peppers

serves 4

6 large garlic cloves, unpeeled

400 g/14 oz bottled roasted red peppers, drained and sliced

200 g/7 oz canned chopped tomatoes

3 tbsp olive oil

¼ tsp dried chilli flakes

1 tsp chopped fresh oregano or thyme, plus extra sprigs to garnish

350 g/12 oz dried tagliatelle

salt and pepper

Preheat the oven to 200°C/400°F/Gas Mark 6. Place the unpeeled garlic cloves in a shallow, ovenproof dish. Roast in the preheated oven for 7–10 minutes, until the garlic cloves feel soft.

Put the peppers, tomatoes and oil in a food processor or blender, then purée. Squeeze the garlic flesh into the purée. Add the chilli flakes and oregano. Season to taste with salt and pepper. Blend again, then scrape into a saucepan and set aside.

Bring a large saucepan of lightly salted water to the boil. Add the pasta, bring back to the boil and cook for 8–10 minutes, or until tender but still firm to the bite. Drain and transfer to a warmed serving dish.

Reheat the sauce and pour over the pasta. Toss well to mix, garnish with sprigs of oregano and serve immediately.

Fettuccine with Peppers & Olives

serves 4

100 ml/3½ fl oz olive oil

1 onion, finely chopped

200 g/7 oz black olives, stoned and coarsely chopped

400 g/14 oz canned chopped tomatoes, drained

2 red, yellow or orange peppers, deseeded and cut into thin strips

350 g/12 oz dried fettuccine

salt and pepper

freshly grated pecorino cheese, to serve

Heat the oil in a large, heavy-based saucepan. Add the onion and cook over a low heat, stirring occasionally, for 5 minutes, or until softened. Add the olives, tomatoes and peppers and season to taste with salt and pepper. Cover and simmer gently over a very low heat, stirring occasionally, for 35 minutes.

Meanwhile, bring a large, heavy-based saucepan of lightly salted water to the boil. Add the pasta, return to the boil and cook for 8–10 minutes, or until tender but still firm to the bite. Drain the pasta and transfer to a warmed serving dish.

Spoon the sauce onto the pasta and toss well. Sprinkle generously with the pecorino cheese and serve immediately.

Penne with Mixed Beans

serves 4

1 tbsp olive oil

1 onion, chopped

1 garlic clove, finely chopped

1 carrot, finely chopped

1 celery stick, finely chopped

425 g/15 oz canned mixed beans, drained and rinsed

225 ml/8 fl oz passata

1 tbsp chopped fresh chervil, plus extra leaves to garnish

350 g/12 oz dried penne

salt and pepper

Heat the oil in a large, heavy-based frying pan. Add the onion, garlic, carrot and celery and cook over a low heat, stirring occasionally, for 5 minutes, or until the onion has softened.

Add the mixed beans, passata and chopped chervil to the frying pan and season the mixture to taste with salt and pepper. Cover and simmer gently for 15 minutes.

Meanwhile, bring a large, heavy-based saucepan of lightly salted water to the boil. Add the pasta, return to the boil and cook for 8–10 minutes, or until tender but still firm to the bite. Drain the pasta and transfer to a warmed serving dish. Add the mixed bean sauce, toss well and serve immediately, garnished with extra chervil.